GROW YOUR OWN
TOMATOES

BY LISA J. AMSTUTZ

PEBBLE
a capstone imprint

Published by Pebble, an imprint of Capstone
1710 Roe Crest Drive, North Mankato, Minnesota 56003
capstonepub.com

Copyright © 2025 by Capstone. All rights reserved. No part of this publication may be reproduced in whole or in part, or stored in a retrieval system, or transmitted in any form or by any means, electronic, mechanical, photocopying, recording, or otherwise, without written permission of the publisher.

Library of Congress Cataloging-in-Publication Data is available on the Library of Congress website.
ISBN: 9780756589516 (hardcover)
ISBN: 9780756589776 (paperback)
ISBN: 9780756589554 (ebook PDF)

Summary: Step-by-step instructions and paired photographs show readers how to grow and care for a tomato plant. A recipe along with a simple explanation of plant growth furthers learning.

Editorial Credits
Editor: Erika L. Shores; Designer: Heidi Thompson; Media Researcher: Jo Miller; Production Specialist: Tori Abraham

Image Credits
Shutterstock: Alina Red, cover (seedling), 13 (seedling), Anuta23, 5, BW Folsom, 6-7 (soil), Carolyn Franks, 6 (tape), Danny Smythe, 6 (trowel), Gold Picture, 7 (stake), Happy TX, 18, Hasibul_Zero, cover (middle, tape), 11 (tape), 12 (tape), HstrongART, 12 (background), Hunter Leader, 11 (sun), 23 (sun), Hurst Photo, cover (spray bottle), 7(spray bottle), liliya Vantsura, cover (soil cup), 10, 11 (soil cup), 12 (soil cup), 13 (soil cup) 15, Mallinka1, 23 (raindrops), margaryta, 7 (water), Marina Lohrbach, 17, MICRO.S, 6 (seeds), Pixel-Shot, 21, Rinto Kusuma, 7 (string), Ruslan Semichev, cover (empty cup), 6 (cups), 11 (empty cup), 12 (empty cup), Strawberry Blossom, 9, Tim UR, back cover, 1, Trong Nguyen, 19 (left), Valentin Valkov, cover (right), VikiVector, 23 (bottom), Yuriy Korzhenevskyy, 19 (right)

The publisher and the author shall not be liable for any damages allegedly arising from the information in this book, and they specifically disclaim any liability from the use or application of any of the contents of this book.

Any additional websites and resources referenced in this book are not maintained, authorized, or sponsored by Capstone. All product and company names are trademarks™ or registered® trademarks of their respective holders.

Printed and bound in China. 6097

TABLE OF CONTENTS

Grow Your Own! 4

What You Need 6

What You Do 8

Take It Further 20

Behind the Science 22

Glossary 24

About the Author 24

Words in **BOLD** are in the glossary.

GROW YOUR OWN!

Tomatoes come in many colors and sizes. Some are as big as a softball. Others are the size of your thumb. But they all taste good!

You can grow tomatoes at home. It is best to start them indoors. Then move them to a garden. No space? Grow them in a pot on your patio.

WHAT YOU NEED

- tomato seeds
- two clear plastic cups
- **trowel**
- tape
- potting soil
- clean spray bottle
- water
- a sunny garden spot
- **stake**
- string

WHAT YOU DO

STEP 1

Tomato plants grow best in warm soil. Check the **frost date** for your area. You can find this online. Now count back four to six weeks. This is a good time to plant seeds.

STEP 2

Put potting soil into one plastic cup. Leave about 1 inch (2.5 centimeters) of space at the top. Press three seeds into the soil. Water the seeds until the soil is damp.

Put the other cup on top. Tape one side of the cups together. Now you have a mini greenhouse!

11

STEP 3

Set the cups in a sunny spot. Check the seeds each day. Soon they will **sprout.**

Wait until leaves start to grow.
Then you can take off the top cup.
Pick one strong plant to keep.
Pull out any others.

STEP 4

Let the plant grow until it is 6 inches (15 cm) tall. Now it is ready to move outside.

Set the plant out for a few hours each day. Then bring it back in. Do this for a week.

STEP 5

Find a sunny garden spot. Dig a hole about 4 inches (10 cm) deep. Gently pull the plant out of its cup. Keep the soil with it.

Set the plant in the hole. Press soil around it. Water it well.

STEP 6

Take care of your plant. Pull weeds around it. Pick off any pests. **Hornworms** can harm plants. Other bugs can too.

You may need to tie your plant to a stake. This keeps it from falling over.

Soon the plant will **bloom**. Each flower makes a tomato. Wait until the tomatoes are **ripe**. Now they are ready to eat and share.

TAKE IT FURTHER

Fresh tomatoes are great in salads.
You can also try making this fresh salsa.
Ask an adult to help.

- 4 tomatoes, chopped
- 1 pepper, chopped
- 1 tablespoon cilantro, chopped
- 1 tablespoon onion, chopped
- 2 teaspoons lime juice

Stir ingredients together in a bowl.
Add salt to taste. Serve with chips. Yum!

BEHIND THE SCIENCE

Do you make your own lunch? Plants do! But they don't eat food like we do. They make their own.

Plants take in light, water, air, and **nutrients.** They use these to make sugars. This food makes the plant grow.

GLOSSARY

bloom (BLOOM)—to flower

frost date (FROST DAYT)—the date when the last frost comes in an area

hornworm (HORN-wurm)—a caterpillar that feeds on tomato plants

nutrients (NOO-tree-uhnts)—parts of food, like vitamins, that are used for growth

ripe (RIPE)—ready to pick and eat

sprout (SPROUT)—to start to grow

stake (STAYK)—a thick, pointed post

trowel (TROU-uhl)—a tool used to scoop up soil

ABOUT THE AUTHOR

Lisa J. Amstutz is the author of more than 150 children's books on topics ranging from applesauce to zebra mussels. An ecologist by training, she enjoys sharing her love of nature with kids. Lisa lives on a small farm with her family.